still struggling

Paul Hill

DayOne

Copyright © Day One Publications 1997

First printed 1997

Scripture quotations are from The New Kings James Version

ISBN 0 902 548 77 8

Published by Day One Publications

6 Sherman Road, Bromley, Kent BR1 3JH

Designed by Steve Devane and printed by Clifford Frost Ltd, Wimbledon SW19 2SE

Dead, yet still speaking

'Gilbert and Sullivan' said the old lady, 'I've heard of them! Aren't they film stars?' Those remarks, addressed to me many years ago, may bring a smile to your face, but I want to consider ignorance which is much more serious. Sadly, many Christians know very little about stirring events without which there would be little or no evangelical faith in our land today. I refer to the Protestant Reformation. What do you know about the heroism of men like William Tyndale, Hugh Latimer and John Bunyan, who lived and died during one of the most glorious periods in the history of God's Church?

Perhaps the word 'history' recalls unhappy memories of boring lessons at school, and tempts you to agree with the American industrialist Henry T. Ford, that 'History is bunk!' But is it? What 'pop' fan would be unaware of Elvis or the Beatles? What lover of classical music would know almost nothing about Mozart or Beethoven? What cricket enthusiast is ignorant of Grace, Hobbs or Bradman?

If a non-Christian knows much about the history of their particular interest, how sad if the child of God cares little about the dramatic story of the body of Christ in a hostile world, the Church for which He bled and died. Our Protestant forefathers had such a high view of the Church that they would have been grieved by the ignorance which characterises much of the evangelicalism of our day.

Why this change of attitude? One reason may be the impact of that strand of prophetical teaching which implies that the Church Age is a small interval between two periods of Jewish superiority. In addition, with the rise of Darwinism and modern criticism of the Bible, many evangelicals lost interest in their spiritual roots. Church history was for academics and of little contemporary relevance; the prime concern was to win souls and anything which distracted from that must be avoided. In the sixteenth century, God raised up men who did not believe that 'the winning of souls' was more important than the Reformation of the Church.

Whatever the reasons, many of today's Christians have lost that concern for the purity of God's Church which was once the hallmark of His people. How many young people are 'called' to Bible College or Christian work with scarcely a reference to the leadership of their local fellowship? How many Christian organisations appear to function independently of the local church? We even hear, from so-called evangelicals that the Reformation was a mistake! Those who agree should recall the last words of Hugh Latimer to his fellow martyr Nicholas Ridley, 'Be of good comfort Master Ridley, and play the man. We shall this day light such a candle, by God's grace, in England, as I trust shall never be put out.'

We read: 'Whatsoever things were written aforetime were written for our learning, that we through patience and comfort of the scriptures might have hope.'[1] Something similar could be said about the Reformation. We can learn much from our evangelical ancestors, because many of our problems confronted them.

Those that maintain that they need only the Bible and the Holy Spirit, need to remember that God has ordained that the Church should be fed by teachers and pastors. If we need them, and the fellowship of our fellow believers, we need more than the Bible and the Holy Spirit to help us grow as Christians. If we can learn from today's teachers, can we not learn from the giants of yesterday, who in turn admitted their debt to their forefathers? As we shall see Martin Luther was assisted by the experience of Jan Huss. Great preachers like George Whitefield and Charles Spurgeon found the writings of precious generations invaluable. Yet today, some people claim to have no such needs!

There is a further reason why we should take an interest in these events. Many of the men and women we shall consider suffered terribly, some laying down their lives for the gospel. Such heroism has given us the precious gift of freedom of worship. We owe it to these martyrs and to coming generations to seek to preserve this liberty. Finally, remember that the Christian Church is the Church of God! The Reformation is the story of what God has done. It is glorifying to God. We are on earth to glorify God. How can a Christian be bored with or disinterested in what God has done! Do we glorify God by remaining ignorant of His story?

Preface

Almost twenty years ago I gave a series of talks entitled 'Our Protestant Heritage.' John Blanchard suggested that they could be the basis for a book. Having written the introduction, the idea died. Two years ago I repeated those talks, receiving further encouragement from John to put pen to paper, which I have done.

I acknowledge the invaluable help I have received from John Blanchard, Robert Oliver, Oliver Rice, Rachel Batten as well as the General Secretary and Publications Committee of Day One Publications. Without their assistance this book would have remained an idea.

Paul Hill

When I was at school, I found history – even the history of my own country and our nearest continent – boring and pointless. What could possibly be gained from understanding the issues which lay behind such a confusing cocktail of wars and rebellions, treaties and laws, parliaments and persecutions?

What a costly mistake I made! Winston Churchill once said, 'To test the present, you must appeal to history,' and I have long since come to see that we can never have a proper understanding of where we are until we realise how we got here.

This is especially true from a Christian perspective, and it is vitally important for believers to have a clear grasp of their religious heritage. In the 2000 years that have passed since New Testament times, no period has been more dramatic or decisive than the 16th Century. There were times when genuine Christianity seemed to be hanging by its fingernails and in danger of being swept into oblivion, smothered by a cruel and corrupt religious dictatorship. Its survival called for amazing courage and cost countless lives, and this fascinating study weaves together some of the key events which shaped the development of those turbulent years.

We should be grateful to Paul Hill for this excellent sketch of some of the most heroic events in our nation's church history, and I warmly commend it to a new generation of Christians in the hope that it will encourage them to uncover their past, learn its lessons, and emulate the spiritual giants and countless 'unknowns' whose faithfulness purchased the gospel freedom we enjoy today.

John Blanchard

❶ The German Giant

The last day of October is Reformation Day. On this day, in 1517, Martin Luther, a German monk, nailed 95 theses to the door of 'All Saints' the Castle Church in Wittenberg. The Reformation had begun. Or had it? This was a vital event, but it would be misleading to suggest that the Reformation began on a particular day.

There had long been a growing demand for reform of the Church but little agreement as to what changes were needed, or indeed how they could be carried out. For most, what was needed was either administrative, social or moral reform, rather than doctrinal change.

It is important to realise that there was only one recognised Church throughout much of Europe – the Roman Catholic church, and that to be outside of it was to be outside of salvation itself. The climate for change was concerned with improving the structure, efficiency and image of the Church, not challenging its universal authority.

There were evangelicals at this time, but they were usually outside the church. When they emerged from within, they suffered for their convictions. In England, John Wycliffe (1329–84) – whose followers were known as the lollards – was excommunicated, whilst remaining within the Catholic system. In 1415, Jan Hus having also been excommunicated, died at the stake in Prague. Luther's protests resulted in people breaking away from the Catholic Church. Initially Luther did not associate himself with either of these men. But a climate of change was moving across Europe in a way which was to help Luther considerably, and which was to give him a distinct advantage over Wycliffe and Huss. By 1517 there was a growing sense of antagonism towards both the Church and the clergy. To make matters worse for Rome, many European countries experienced a shift towards a greater sense of national identity, returning power back to the state and away from Rome, with consequential decrease in Papal authority.

It was also a time of new ideas, particularly of humanism, which resulted in many people questioning traditional beliefs and values. There was also a new technology. The discovery of printing meant that for the first time new ideas could circulate widely and quickly. These factors were to be of enormous assistance both to Luther and his successors.

Martin Luther had become a Catholic priest in 1507. In 1510 he went on a religious pilgrimage to Rome which reinforced his disillusionment with the Church. Von Staupitz, the local Vicar-General of the Augustinians, a very strict religious order, was sympathetic towards Luther's reservations, and appointed him a lecturer in Biblical studies at Wittenburg University, near Berlin. Luther began to study the Psalms, Romans and Galations. In his book, 'Here I stand,' Roland Bainton points out that when Luther reflected upon Psalm 22, he wondered much about the sufferings of Christ. As Bainton puts it, 'Christ too had Anfechtungen.' In other words, Christ experienced some of the same feelings that Luther had. He too felt anguish. He too felt himself to have been abandoned and forsaken by God. But how could this be when Christ was pure? Luther came to see in Bainton's words, that 'wrath and love fuse upon the cross.' Luther had been acutely aware both of his failings and of God's wrath, and had no peace or assurance. Nothing that the Church offered made any difference. It began to dawn on him that God was not only holy and angry with sin, but also gracious. Continuing with his studies, especially in Romans, he came to understand what Paul meant by justification by faith. Salvation, he discovered, was not by faith in what the Church did nor by what he himself could do, but by faith in what Christ did, when he died in Luther's place for Luther's sin. When he grasped this he was overwhelmed and wrote:

> *Thereupon I felt myself to be reborn and to have gone through open doors into paradise. The whole of Scripture took on a new meaning, and whereas before the 'justice of God' had filled me with hate, now it became to me inexpressibly sweet in greater love. This passage of Paul became to me a gate to heaven...*

At this time the church had financial difficulties. The Pope decided to introduce a scheme under which it was claimed that a person's sentence in purgatory could be reduced if their relatives or family made a cash contribution to the church funds in the form of a 'plenary indulgence' sold by travelling monks. A rhyme employed by one monk called Tetzel aptly sums up the principle: 'as soon as the coin in the coffer rings, the soul from purgatory springs.' Luther was outraged and was convinced that if the Pope knew of it, he would intervene. It was this issue which led Luther to nail those 95 Theses to the door of the Church in Wittenburg. They are an attack against the system of indulgences rather than of the Pope or the Church. It is clear that at this point, he did not accept the final authority of the Scriptures.

Luther was reported to the Pope and summonded to appear before Cardinal Cajetan. When challenged, Luther bravely refuted the authority of the Pope over Scripture, a position which he developed over the years.

A year later, he was sent to face John Eck, a professor from the University of Ingolstadt who Luther found to be a formidable and skilful opponent. Eck accused Luther of following the 'heresies' of Wycliffe and Hus. He denied this, but during an interval, he made use of the library and discovered that he actually shared many of the views of Hus, who had, in common with Luther, been influenced by Augustine, an early Church father.

As a result of this discovery, Luther admitted that there was a connection, but argued that it was for the sake of Scripture that we should reject popes and councils. Incensed by this, Eck asked, 'Except for you is all the Church in error?' Try to imagine what that meant for Luther. Was the rest of the Church wrong and had it been so for centuries? Was Luther the only one who understood? Many of us have had the same familiar questions thrown our way, 'How do you know that you are right?' 'Why should so many others be wrong?' Despite this challenge, Luther stood firm – and was excommunicated.

In 1521 he was summoned to the Diet of Worms (a diet was an important church council) where he made his famous statement:

> *Unless I am convicted by Scripture and plain reason – I do not accept the authority of popes and councils, for they contradicted each other – my conscience is captive to the Word of God. I cannot and I will not recant any-thing, for to go against conscience is neither right nor safe. God help me. Amen.*

Luther went into exile. While he was in hiding, evangelical reforms were introduced in Wittenburg; private masses were abolished; for the first time, Communion wine was drunk not only by the priests, but by the whole congregation. The Mass was celebrated not in Latin, but, for the first time, in the language of the people – German. Priests dressed in ordinary clothes rather than traditional elaborate vestments. The time honoured tradition of celebrating masses for the dead in order to petition for the early release of their souls from purgatory was ended. The imposed celibacy rule was lifted from both priests and nuns. In church buildings, religious icons and statues were either removed or smashed. Not everyone agreed with such radical changes. Violence resulted and chaos reigned. At great risk, Luther returned to Wittenburg under cover. He advised his fellow reformers, 'Preach, pray but do not fight.'

Luther was an extraordinary man. I have described him as the German hammer because of his unique contribution in demolishing the almost universal power of Rome. Yet he was also cautious and conservative. He adopted a middle way between Catholicism and what later became known as Calvinism. Other Reformers were to argue that the authority of Scripture meant that the Church's worship should adopt 'only what Scripture commands.' Luther conversely allowed 'only what Scripture does not condemn.' Yet, whatever our reservations about some of his actions and opinions, we should honour Luther as a man greatly used of God for the advancement of biblical truth and Christian freedom. Others were to build upon his foundation and what they built is still growing today.

❷ The French Rapier

Martin Luther and John Calvin were, humanly speaking, the two great pillars of the Reformation. Yet how diffferent they were! Luther was the hammer; the demolisher, the prophet; while Calvin was the scholar; the rapier, the builder; the theologian. He was one of the most remarkable men in Western Society, to such an extent that his thinking spread beyond the realms of theology, influencing the development of Capitalism, Modern Science and Constitutional Democracy. Yet he is also one of the most misunderstood, misrepresented and maligned men in both secular and religious terms. If ever there was a man whose impact demonstrated that the natural man does not receive the things of the Spirit of God, it was John Calvin!

The story of his life is less spectacular and dramatic than that of Luther. He was born in 1509 and educated in Paris. He was gifted and self-disciplined and was taught to oppose Wycliffe, Hus and Luther. He was converted in his early twenties and soon identified himself with the Reformed cause. The dangers led him to leave France for Basle in Switzerland where he devoted himself to the study of the Scriptures and the Early Fathers, culminating in his 'Institutes of the Christian Religion' which he completed when he was twenty six. Never before had a young Christian written such a profound or comprehensive work.

In 1535, while in Geneva, Calvin met William Farel, who was the spiritual leader of the Reformed church. Farel recognised Calvin as the ideal man for the task of building up the Church and he was appointed as 'Reader in Holy Scripture to the Church in Geneva.'

Like Luther before him and many after him, Calvin experienced fierce opposition as soon as he began to introduce evangelical reforms. After nearly two years of fruitful ministry, the city leaders ordered him out and Calvin went on to Strasbourg where he was received favourably, and where the church grew. But pastoral triumph was matched by personal tragedy; he lost a premature child and his wife died some time later.

In 1541, he reluctantly returned to Geneva, where he remained until his death in 1564. The Church there was in disarray, and he saw not only the need for preaching and the sacraments but also for Church discipline. Here, he differed from Luther who took the view that once the word had preached, the seed which had been sowed would bear fruit by the power of the Holy Spirit. Calvin placed an additional emphasis on maintaining Church order with a vision of a fellowship of saints with internal spiritual discipline which even included excommunication for spiritual offences.

How was such discipline to be exercised? Calvin saw four offices in the New Testament Church: pastors, teachers, elders and deacons, of which the last two were occupied by what we now call 'lay' people. The offices of teacher and Pastor were to be separate and distinct. Teachers were responsible for interpreting and teaching, whereas pastors had additional responsibilities of discipline and administering the sacraments. Few Christians, today, maintain that distinction. Elders were responsible for the 'care of souls' while deacons had special responsibility for the sick and poor. Pastors, teachers and elders met regularly to discuss both moral and doctrinal issues. Those accused of committing an offence were called before the leaders and encouraged to repent. If they refused they were excommunicated until they demonstrated a change of heart.

Inevitably there were problems. The underlying difficulty appeared to be in the widely held assumption that Geneva was a Christian society. But it was obviously not a voluntary fellowship of believers. Not everyone agreed with John Knox, the Scottish Reformer, that this was 'the most perfect school of Christ that ever was on earth since the days of the apostles.' As a result, opposition was predictable, especially from those who were neither regenerate nor spiritual but were being expected to live under a demanding biblical ethic without the God-given desire to do so or ability of the Holy Spirit to live up to scriptural demands.

The tension inevitably put Calvin under great pressure and like all of us, his record was not unblemished. Much has been written about the incident of a man called Servetus, who was sentenced to death for heresy. The Reformed Churches in Switzerland were unanimous in supporting this action but, while Calvin agreed with the verdict, he did not endorse the method of execution. It is easy for us, centuries later, to judge events by today's standards. Had Calvin believed that Church and State were two distinct bodies, he might have argued for Servetus to be expelled from the Church, rather than to be executed.

When Calvin died in 1564, he might have been disappointed at the immediate response in Geneva, but his influence was to spread to the Low Countries, Scotland, England and the New World. Apart from his indirect impact upon politics, science and economics, Calvin was the theologian of the Reformation. He gave the evangelicals a far greater awareness of the co-equality of the three persons in the Godhead. He developed their understanding of the ministries of our Lord as Prophet, Priest and King. He placed great emphasis upon Scripture as the only source of revelation for a true knowledge of God. He wrote commentaries on nearly every book in the Bible, and preached several hundred sermons a year.

Today, the very mention of his name triggers mistrust in an age which largely shuns 'election' and 'predestination.' Consequently, many people now choose to completely ignore all his works, rejecting him entirely. Yet some people, with limited theological knowledge, dismiss him and his teaching.

Calvin's views on these controversial subjects were similar to those of many evangelicals from John Wycliffe through to George Whitefield. Yet it was his belief in the sovereign power of the Holy Spirit in salvation that was Calvin's greatest contribution to an understanding of biblical teaching. For centuries, the Church had taught that salvation came through the administering of the sacraments. Calvin rediscovered that God gives it freely to man directly through his Spirit.

As for predestination, the American writer B.B. Warfield comments that it 'is not the root from which Calvinism springs, but one of the branches which it has inevitably thrown out.' Warfield was arguing that the bible has consistently taught that salvation depends ultimately upon God. One of the branches stemming from that view of salvation is predestination. Calvin's critics take it to be the root. Speaking of the Reformation and the gospel, Warfield says that Luther answered the question, 'What must I do to be saved?', whereas Calvin goes further and answers the question, 'And from whence did that salvation come?'

The answer is, from God. How do Calvin's 'Institutes' begin? They begin with God. How does salvation begin? It too begins with God. Here is the heart of Calvin's theology, which included the bedrock truth that salvation is a miracle which begins with God. Man is not a cripple in need of a remedy, but a corpse in need of a resurrection. God doesn't help a man to be saved, but saves a helpless man. God doesn't influence man, he intervenes in man. Men, who are spiritually dead, cannot help God to perform miracles – and regeneration is a miracle.

What about the so-called 'Five Points of Calvinism'? These were formulated about 50 years after Calvin's death, in response to five points put forward by the Dutch theologian Jacobus Arminius and which were opposed by all the Reformed Churches. The Synod of Dort (1618) confirmed Calvin's position and stated what has been generally accepted as the Reformed view ever since. A majority of Protestant churches embraced this 'Calvinistic' view of salvation, which, according to the great 19th century English preacher Charles Spurgeon, was but a 'nickname for the gospel.'

As with the German 'hammer' so with the French 'rapier' we bless God for these servants who were used to restore the truth of the original gospel. The quality of the man is revealed by his Will which includes these moving words:

'In the first place I render thanks to God, not only because he has had compassion on me, his poor creature, to draw me out of the abyss of idolatry on which I was plunged, in order to bring me to the light of his gospel and make me a partaker of the doctrine of salvation, of which I was altogether unworthy, and continuing his mercy he has supported me amid so many sins and shortcomings, which were such that I deserved to be rejected by him a hundred thousand times – but what is more, he has so far extended his mercy towards me as to make use of me and of my labour, to convey and announce the truth of his gospel; protesting that it is my wish to live and die in this faith which he has bestowed upon me, having no other hope for refuge except in his gratuitous adoption, upon which all my salvation is founded; embracing the grace which he has given me in our Lord Jesus Christ, and accepting the merits of his death and passion, in order that by this means all my sins may be buried; and praying him so to wash and cleanse me by the blood of this great Redeemer, which has been shed for us poor sinners, that I may appear before his face, bearing as it were his image.'

The following comment on the influence of John Calvin, made by Theodore Beza, Calvin's successor in Geneva, is not an exaggeration:

'It has pleased God to show us, in the life of a single man of our time, how to live and how to die.'..... Now there's a testimony!

❸ The English Candle

Turning from the Continent to England, what was the country's spiritual condition before the Reformation? According to J.C.Ryle, the first Bishop of Liverpool, dense religious ignorance, degrading super-stition and rampant unholiness dominated the country and paralysed the church. Ryles' classic book, 'Five English Reformers', published by the Banner of Truth Trust, paints a vivid and detailed picture.

How did the Reformation in England change all this? There is a popular view that Henry VIII's divorce of Catherine of Aragon was the main reason for the Reformation, but this is untrue since Henry remained a Roman Catholic. The main consequence of the divorce was that Henry – not the Pope-was to be the head of the Church in England. One contemporary writer, Iain Murray has summed it up: 'In the trans-formation that took place ... we must look at men only as secondary causes; the deliverance of the land came from a Sovereign hand.'

William Tyndale was one of these 'secondary causes.' At a time when God's word could be read only in Latin, many of the clergy's poor fluency resulted in a complete ignorance of even basic Biblical teaching. Tyndale longed for the day when all people – from the clergy to the least educated – would be able to read and understand God's word in their own native tongue. He declared, 'If God spare my life, ere many years, I will cause a boy that driveth the plough shall know more of the Scripture than thou dost.' His evangelical preaching aroused such fierce opposition that in 1524 he was forced to flee to the Continent where he continued with his work of translating the Scriptures. In 1526, the first copies of his English New Testament were smuggled into England. Eventually he was betrayed into the hands of his enemies and in 1536 was both strangled and burnt. His dying words, 'Lord, open the King of England's eyes' were not in vain; two years later, a royal decree required a copy of the Bible – in English – to be placed in every parish church in the land. Brian Edwards has written a fine biography of Tyndale, entitled 'God's Outlaw', published by Evangelical Press.

The persecution that Tyndale suffered was set to continue. In 1531, Bilney and Byfield were burnt to death. Byfield was accused of buying copies of Tyndale's New Testament on the Continent. When asked, 'With what intent did you bring into the country the errors of Luther?' he gave this stirring reply, 'To make the gospel known ... and to glorify God before the people.' Frith came back from abroad, having been promised a safe return, but was arrested and executed in 1533. Bilney, Byfield, Bainham, Lambert and Frith all died for the gospel. These statistics alone dispel the popular misconception that Henry VIII started the reformation. The fact was that Henry was no Reformer!

In 1533, Thomas Cranmer became Archbishop of Canterbury. Despite good intentions, he was often frustrated by what he saw as ungodly Bishops who were reluctant to see through reforms because of vested interests. Luther commented: 'I have done more in four weeks than these Englishmen in twelve years.' In 1539 'Six Articles' enforcing Romanism were published. Hugh Latimer protested and was arrested. Garret, Jerome and Barnes were martyred at Smithfield. Others were arrested; some fled the country. These were dark days for lovers of the gospel, but, as Iain Murray has said, 'Tyndale had done something which could not be withstood. The Scriptures, like a mighty river, carrying the living waters of the gospel, had been let loose.'

In 1547 Edward VI became King. Thanks to Thomas Cranmer there were sweeping changes. The Lord's Supper replaced the Mass; clergy were allowed to marry; a new Prayer Book was introduced, and exiles such as Hooper returned to become Bishops. In 1552, a more Protestant Prayer Book followed. The altar was replaced by the table, priests were replaced by ministers, and the Roman vestments, tradionally worn by the clergy, were forbidden. Sadly, however, Edward's brief reign was soon ended. His dying prayer is remarkable, especially from a sixteen year old:

> *'Lord I commend my spirit to Thee. O Thou, my Lord,
> how happy and blessed would be my condition if I were
> with Thee! But for the sake of Thy elect preserve my life
> and restore me to my former health, that I may be able
> faithfully to serve Thee. Ah, my Lord, be kind and gra-
> cious to Thy people, and save the Kingdom of Thy inheri-
> tance! Ah Lord God, preserve They elect people of
> England! Ah my Lord God, defend this, Thy realm and
> protect it from Popery, and maintain the true religion and
> pure worship of Thy name, that I and my people may be
> .... to praise and celebrate Thy holy name. Amen.'*

Although it may have seemed at the time that God ignored that prayer, we can now see otherwise!

Edward was succeeded by Mary, and in a very short time Romanism was vigorously restored. Bibles were removed and burnt. Students at Cambridge were ordered not to 'keep, hold, maintain and defend any opinion erroneous, or error of Wycliffe, Huss and Luther.' Instead, they were to believe only what the Catholic Church taught 'concerning faith and works, grace and freewill.' Dissenting bishops were imprisoned and a total of 288 Protestant men, women and children were martyred. When Bishop John Hooper was told that life was sweet and death was bitter, he replied, 'Eternal life is more sweet and eternal death is more bitter.' When facing a martyr's death, Rowland Taylor declared, 'Good people I have taught you nothing but God's Holy Word, and these lessons that I have taken out of the Bible, and I am come hither to seal it with my blood.'

Others were equally fearless as they sealed their own testimonies in blood. Bradford stated: 'Be of good comfort, brother, for we shall have a merry supper with the Lord this night.' Philpott asked: 'Shall I disdain to suffer at this stake, seeing my Redeemer did not refuse to suffer a most vile death on the cross for me?' We have already noted Latimer's distinguished comment about lighting a candle in England that would never be put out. To God's praise, the candle still burns today!

Ryle's account of the martyrdom of Bishop Hooper is a fitting conclusion to this section. Not only is it a stirring example of courage and a challenge to our faith, but it also illustrates that the English

Reformers were not martyrs for an opinion or an interpretation. They were at the stake because the gospel was at stake.

Before Hooper died, a box allegedly containing a pardon was placed in front of him. If he would change his mind the pardon would be his, but his response was crisp and clear: 'If you love my soul, away with it.' Near Tyndale's statue on the Thames Embankment, there was a notice which read, 'Keep to the path.' Were Tyndale to return he would undoubtedly tell us, 'Keep to the path – of the Protestant Reformation.'

❹ The English Flame

Changes in the monarchy during these reforming years led to a pendulem swing of extremes; whereas Edward was distinctly evangelical, Mary had been a staunch defender of the Catholic faith. When Elizabeth succeeded Mary in 1558, she decided to take the 'via media', a middle way between Geneva and Rome.

Many Protestant exiles returned, hoping that England might again become evangelical. But when the Act of Supremacy of 1559 elevated the Sovereign to the position of Head of the Church, the Protestants decided upon passive resistance. They had their first clash over the appointment of bishops. Some of the returning exiles declined to accept positions because the Queen was empowered to make the appointments herself. Others accepted, but found that they had to compromise in the process. Lord Burghley made a telling observation, 'I fear the places alter men.' Sadly that still rings true today!

Between 1563-67 the Vestiarian Controversy raged. Under new rules, the clergy were to wear the surplice and square cap which, for the more consistent Protestants, was an unhappy reminder of Mary's reign. Within the mood of compromise, some dismissed it as 'a thing indifferent.' Others could not, leading to the first movements towards independence and separatism.

Edward Dering and Thomas Cartwright raised more radical voices. Bishops, they said, should have a solely spiritual function, and the

Church should be governed by a presbytery, with each parish electing its own minister. Dering was suspended and Cartwright fled. It was about this time that those who wanted to make the Church more Protestant and Reformed acquired the nickname of 'Puritans'.

Although initially this title was used for those who wanted to 'purify' the Church, it later gained a wider use.

The Puritans sought reform by Parliament. A Bill declaring that the Prayer Book was 'an imperfect book ... out of the Popish dunghill' was surrendered to the Queen! Field and Wilcox went further and attacked the whole structure of the Church. They wanted a Confession of Faith and a form of discipline based upon the Geneva model. Bishops were no longer assumed to be brothers! Field declared, 'We in England are so far off from having a Church rightly reformed according to God's Word that as yet we are not come to the outward face of the same.' Field and Wilcox were put in Newgate Prison.

In 1576 Grindal became Archbishop of Canterbury. The Queen wanted to put an end to the Puritan 'prophesying' Conferences, but Grindal was a man of courage and conviction. He dared to suggest that the Queen should refer such matters to the bishops, telling her, 'Though ye are a mighty Prince, yet remember He which dwelleth in heaven is mightier.' Grindal remained resolute and was suspended from office by Elizabeth from 1577-1582. He died from ill health. More separatism followed, but while Robert Browne and Harrison also joined Cartwright in Holland, most Puritans remained to form 'a Church within a Church.'

In 1576 a radical Presbyterian Bill was defeated in Parliament and six Puritan leaders were imprisoned. Two of the best known were Greenwood and Barrow. They urged separatism, asserting that The Anglican Church was not truly a Church at all according to the Biblical model, but a mixture of believers and unbelievers. The Church, they insisted, needed to be a voluntary fellowship of believers. Barrow argued: 'There may none be admitted into the Church of Christ but such enter by public profession of the true faith.' He strongly opposed the law which made the nation nominally Christian, and ridiculed the idea that: 'All this people, ... were in one day, with the blast of Queen Elizabeth's trumpet ... made faithful Christians and true professors.'

The separatists became increasingly critical of those Puritans who remained in a Church whose 19th Article said that 'the visible church of Christ is a congregation of faithful men.'

An anonymous pamphleteer, Martin Marprelate, produced biting satirical tracts against the Church establishment. The reaction was predictably hostile, as radical Puritanism was effectivly outlawed for the rest of Elizabeth's reign.

A new kind of Puritanism emerged. The evangelicals were 'tarrying for the magistrate; or waiting for reform. As for Elizabeth, one writer has said that 'religiously she was in 1603 what she was in 1558; a boulder in the path of Puritanism, unavoidable, insurmountable, unmoveable.' [2] The candle had not been extinguished, the flame was still burning, but the Queen had proved a frustrating obstacle.

When James VI of Scotland became King in 1603, his Presbyterian background gave the Puritans cause for increased hope. Ironically though, he was to prove an even more formidable opponent, making it clear that 'the Puritans should either conform or be harried out of the land.' Puritan congregations from Gainsborough and Scrooby are notable because they did leave the country, departing in 1609 for Leyden in Holland. Later, they formed the basis of the Pilgrim Fathers. Puritanism 'flourished wherever its devotees could avoid the direct gaze of the sovereign.' [3]

The Puritans continued to be suppressed. The reign of James was 'like a morning twilight behind which the great and decisive events of the next reign are slowly awakening.' [4] The flame was to become the furnace.

It may be helpful to say something about Puritanism in general before considering the reigns of Charles I and II. The Westminster Confession of Faith of 1643 stressed the importance of Scripture by which 'it pleased the Lord ... to reveal Himself, and to declare His will unto the Church; and afterwards ... to commit the same wholly unto writing, which maketh the holy Scripture to be most necessary; those former ways of God's revealing His will until His people being now ceased.'

Many Lutherans and Anglicans would have agreed. But the English Puritans and Scottish Presbyterians differed from them in a crucial way; Both accepted the authority of Scripture, but the Puritans – following Calvin – went further and argued that 'nothing should be introduced into the government and worship of the Church unless a positive warrant for it could be found in Scripture.' This view of the Puritans was known as the 'regulative principle.' The issue for them was not a question of whether the Scriptures were true or not, but whether they had authority. The others 'generally held that the Church might warrantably introduce innovations ... which might seem fitted to be useful, provided it could not be shown that there was anything in Scripture which expressly prohibited... them.'

The Westminster Confession, like Calvin's Institutes, began with God. The Puritans had a high view of God. Macaulay, the historian and statesman, sensed this when he wrote:

> 'Not content with acknowledging, in general terms, an overruling providence, they habitually ascribed every event to the will of the Great Being for whose power nothing was too vast, for whose inspection nothing was too minute. To know Him, to serve Him, to enjoy Him, was with them the great end of existence. If they were acquainted with the works of philosophers and poets, they were deeply read in the oracles of God. If their names were not found in the registers or heralds, they were recorded in the Lamb's Book of Life. If their steps were not accompanied by a splendid train of menials, legions of ministering angels had charge of them. The very meanest of them was a being to whose fate a mysterious and terrible importance belonged, on whose slightest of actions the spirits of light and darkness looked with anxious interest, who had been destined, before Heaven and Earth were created, to enjoy a felicity which should continue when Heaven and Earth have passed away.'

It is hard to imagine a better description of the Puritan perspective. The Puritans also emphasised personal holiness. They were fierce opponents of antinomianism – the belief that because we are saved without keeping the law of God, we do not need to keep God's moral commandments. They were not so much opposed to the theatre (as is often imagined) as opposed to its wicked immorality. In some ways they competed against the theatre. They placed great emphasis upon preaching, upon powerful and dramatic, pointed and direct preaching! They rejected stained glass in church buildings and organ music in worship. Nothing was to obscure the biblical message. One Puritan wrote: 'This is the glory of our Churches. Although the walls be not painted, although the vestures be not silk ... although they want their frankincense and organs, yet the Word of the Lord and His Spirit shall stand ... in the midst of them. The gospel of Jesus Christ ringeth in them although their organs cease, that sweet savour of life is felt although that earthly frankincense be put out.'

Like Luther, the Puritans also stressed the importance of each man working at his trade or profession, to the glory of God. A minister or a miller, a teacher or a tailor, each one should apply himself diligently to his calling. This outlook has fascinated those who argue that Puritanism was a powerful stimulus to both the emergence of capitalism and the rise of science in Western society.

The Puritan emphasis upon the Sabbath was another hallmark and has been described as 'the first and perhaps the only important English contribution to the development of Reformed theology in the first century of its history.'[5]

As we have mentioned, Puritans strongly emphasised the importance of preaching the gospel which they regarded as the core of their worship. 'Preaching was the chariot on which salvation comes riding into the hearts of men.'[6] The preachers were plain and practical. They also had a sense of urgency; as Richard Baxter said, 'I preached as never sure to preach again. And as a dying man to dying men.'

The Puritans also emphasised the importance of education and learning, by using the powerful medium of printing 'What had at first been regarded as the pulpit's humble handmaid, became an engine of spiritual war.'[7] During the years of apparent frustration, the Puritan press became a powerful weapon producing literature, which enabled the cause to gain in strength. Someone has written, 'many there were ... quietly sowing the innocent looking dragon's teeth which in time produced Cromwell's iron harvest.'[8]

The world's view of Puritansim is revealing. The Puritans have been ridiculed and misrepresented, yet there has seldom been a more godly group of people since apostolic days. We should glory in them – or rather we should glory in their God and His gospel. They are 'our people.' They are 'our brothers and sisters', of whom the world is not worthy.

❺ The English Furnace

Charles I was the 'first King to have been brought up from childhood as a member of the Church of England. Unlike his predecessors, he regarded the Church of England as the established order. For the first time, the Anglican Church had a Defender of the Faith who had never considered the possibility of defending any other faith.[9] He expected unquestioning obedience to his absolute authority. People were 'to belong with uniform and regular devotion to the Church established by law.' His main instrument in carrying out his policies was Archbishop Laud: 'His ideal was a church rigidly and effectively organised, its services reverently conducted according to a uniform ritual, its hierarchy sagely established, and the whole population gathered together as one docile flock. This vision matched the King's.'[10]

Anglicanism made a significant advance. The Church and the nation were viewed as one allowing no place for independency and non-conformity. As a result, protestantism became more radical. In 1629 Parliament asked the King to surrender his rights to deal with trade, religion and foreign affairs. Charles dissolved parliament marking the start of his personal reign; high Anglican altars were established throughout the realm, and once again the Puritan voice was raised in protest.

In 1635 Charles imposed an unpopular tax called 'The Ship Money', which originated in the Middle Ages and was levied on ports to pay for the protection they gained from the navy. But Charles imposed it on inland towns on the grounds that they also benefited from the navy's protection. As a result, even more people joined the protest movement. In 1639, the Scots were outraged when Laud attempted to re-introduce both the Prayer Book and bishops in Scotland. When Charles recalled

Parliament hoping to gain support for a war against Scotland, he failed. The so-called 'Long Parliament' began with Pym and Hampden in control. Many Puritans who had been imprisoned were released; those who effectively took their places included Laud and The Earl of Strafford.

The Puritans introduced a Bill to curtail the power of bishops, which was carried by eleven votes. A relatively unknown member for Cambridge remarked as he left the House, 'If the Remonstrance had been rejected I would have sold all that I had next morning, and never have seen England any more; and I know there are many honest men of the same resolution.' Oliver Cromwell remained.

In 1642, Episcopal seats in the Lords were abolished, and one year later episcopacy disappeared until the Restoration. Parliament also summoned the now famous Westminster Assembly which drew up a Presbyterian system of worship and church government, in spite of some opposition from Independents. Negotiations between the King and Parliament resulted in Charles agreeing to a Presbyterian form of government. Cromwell and the 'New Model Arm' became influential and the move towards independency began to assert itself. However, Presbyterianism's hopes in England were finally dashed by the Restoration under Charles II. With the monarchy restored, Anglicanism was re-established as the State religion – a bitter blow for the Puritans. In 1662, some 2,000 Puritan ministers renounced their earnings rather than submit to the new Act of Conformity.

These were difficult days for non-conformists. The Passing of the Five Mile Act of 1665 meant that they could not worship within five miles of a city or town, forcing them to meet in the country. Even then they were far from safe, often shaking off their pursuers only by meeting near a county border, so that when threatened, they could cross over to comparative safety. These were the days of John Bunyan, who spent twelve years in Bedford Gaol rather than submit to Anglican liturgy and authority. He may not have been authorised by a bishop but he believed that he was called of God. He would not consent to the Prayer Book authorised by man, but would pray as prompted by the Spirit. In his words, his first avowed intent was to be a pilgrim; nothing could daunt his spirit; he feared not what men said.

Briefly, the Puritans had ruled with Cromwell as Lord Protector. Now they were suffering again. Why had their 'reign' been a failure? Why was the country so glad to see the Monarchy restored?

Many who had been united in war were divided in peace. Cromwell was not as radical as some of his supporters, and he was certainly no democrat. 'The interest of honest man is the interest of the kingdom' he declared. (By honest he meant godly). As for 'the people,' he was concerned 'for their good, not what pleases man.'

Many contemporary commentators have observed that the Puritans' goal was to literally force man into righteousness, by building a society based upon Biblical foundations. The problem with such a scheme was that the majority of people did not have God's law written upon their hearts. The Puritan 'failure' was predictable.

When James II became King in 1685, Romanism was revived and Parliament invited William of Orange to take the throne. What followed has been called, 'The Glorious Revolution.' The Acts of Toleration meant that the non-conformists were given new liberties. They could choose their own pastors and their own places of worship, though it was to be a long time before they could attend universities or take a full part in public life. The 1689 Baptist Confession of Faith would have been impossible before this period.

But this period of non-conformity acted as a catalyst for many alternative beliefs which threatened to eclipse the Reformation, particularly Deism (the idea that God can be discovered by reason and nature and without any special revelation). As someone has remarked, 'God who had been so close to Oliver Cromwell withdrew into the vast recesses of Newtonian space.' That is a caricature, but the evangelical fire burned less brightly until God visited a young man called George Whitefield – but that's another story!

❻ The Scottish Crucible

The story of Scotland's enlightenment is no less compelling. Patrick Hamilton was the first to die for preaching the gospel of grace. His death, in 1523, at the age of twenty four, made a great impact. Other martyrs followed, including George Wishart. In death he declared, 'this fire torments my body, but in no way abates my spirit.' John Knox emerged as a fearless champion of the gospel. In 1557 the evangelicals drew up the first of their Covenants pledging support for one another and for the gospel. Around that time, 82 year old Walter Mill died for the faith, proclaiming defiantly 'a hundred better shall rise out of the ashes of my bones.' By 1560 the Roman Church had all but vanished; the Scottish Parliament said no to the Pope and no to the Mass. The Treaty of Berwick between Scotland and England strengthened the cause of the Reformation.

The Book of Discipline soon followed. This was not only Presbyterian but insisted that the revenues of the Old Church be used for the maintenance of religion, education and the poor. Parliament refused to ratify it!

In 1561 Mary Queen of Scots returned from France. She stood for an alliance with France and Romanism. Knox wanted Presbyterianism and alliance with England. Conflict was inevitable. On her first Sunday a mass was said at Holyrood, to which Knox replied that one mass was more to be feared than 10,000 armed enemies.

In December 1567 new laws meant that the Sovereign must be a Protestant. The Reformed Church was the only National Church. Knox died in 1572. As his body was lowered into the grave, someone commented, 'There lies he who never feared the face of man.'

Andrew Melville became leader of the Protestants telling King James that there were two kingdoms in Scotland, and in the one, James himself was a subject!

The move away from episcopacy was in progress. In 1574 the Church asked, 'Have bishops their function from the Word of God or not!' Two years later the name bishop was common to all who minister to the flock. Melville was told, 'There will never be quiet in this country till half a dozen of you be hanged or banished.' Melville replied, 'It is the same to me whether I rot in the air or the ground, let God be glorified. It will not be in your power to hang or exile his truth.' The 2nd Book of Discipline of 1571 outlawed episcopacy. The first National Covenant of Scotland followed three years later.

The power of the Sovereign in Church Affairs was in jeopardy, as was the financial rewards of the lords.

Melville appeared before the King at Perth. When asked, 'Who dares submit these treasonable articles?' Melville replied, 'We dare' and signed.

An uneasy peace followed, but Melville was accused of seditious and treasonable speeches. He threw his Bible on the table declaring, 'These are my instructions. See if any of you can judge of them.' He fled to Berwick. It became treason to refuse the King's judgement on any matter. For a while the evangelicals were in danger. In 1589 the King left to marry the Princess of Denmark. On his return, six months later, there had been peace, thanks to the efforts of the Church. In 1592, both King and Parliament ratified most of the ideas of the Second Book of Discipline. The great charter of the Church of Scotland was a triumph for the lovers of Reform!

That was not the end of the story. When James VI of Scotland became James I of England, it was not only the English Puritans who were affected. In 1610 bishops were established in Scotland by royal authority. Eight years later the King sought to ensure that worship in Scotland conformed with that of the Anglican Church. Charles I maintained the same policy. In 1637 came a celebrated incident. Rejecting Anglican liturgy, Jenny Geddes threw a stool in St. Giles, in Edinburgh, declaring 'Will ye read that in my lug (ear)?'

In 1638, Presbyterianism was re-established with the signing of the National Covenant. The Solemn League and Covenant followed in 1643. In 1660 the monarchy was restored and troubles returned. Persecution began in 1663. A Covenanter rising was defeated in 1666. Field meetings became treasonable and to preach at them was a capital offence. The Covenanters defeated the Government forces at Drumclog in 1679, but were themselves defeated at Bothwell Bridge and

Ayrsmoss. In 1684-5 came 'The Killing Times' – the worst persecution of all. In 1688 James Renwick became the last of the Covenanter martyrs. With 'The Glorious Revolution', freedom was restored.

Anyone wanting to know more about the story of the Covenanter martyrs, should read 'Fair Sunshine' by Jock Purves. It tells of those who died and of the vital principles for which they laid down their lives. It is impossible to read of such heroic sacrifice and courage, and yet fail to appreciate why they acted as they did. Was it all pointless and unnecessary? Contemporary men governed only by modern ideas might think so. The Covenanter martyrs were men and women who died because they wanted the freedom to worship God without interference from earthly monarchs. They argued that the Church was led by Christ, not by James or Charles. It was not the role of a secular ruler to appoint spiritual leaders in Christ's Church! True worship was not dictated by the rules of an earthly king and his archbishop but according to God's Word.

Let me conclude with some gems from 'Fair Sunshine.' I call them gems because they sparkle with the glory of God. They also warm your heart and challenge you as to the reality of your faith.

Listen to Hugh MacKail. Knowing that he was to die, he shouted: 'Four days now until I see Jesus.' No regret! No self-pity! Climbing the ladder of the scaffold he said: 'Every step is a degree nearer heaven.' Finally he says: 'Now, I leave off to speak anymore to creatures, and turn my speech to thee, O Lord. Now I begin my intercourse with God which shall never be broken off. Farewell, father and mother, friends and relations! Farewell the world and all delights! Farewell, meat and drink! Farewell, sun, moon and stars! Welcome, God and Father! Welcome, sweet Lord Jesus, Mediator of the New Covenant! Welcome, blessed Spirit of grace, God of all consolation! Welcome, glory! Welcome eternal life! Welcome death!'

When James Renwick went to the scaffold he said: 'Lord, I die in the faith that Thou wilt not leave Scotland, but that Thou wilt make the blood of Thy witnesses the seed of Thy church, and return again and glorious in our land. And now, Lord, I am ready; 'the Bride', the Lamb's wife, hath made herself ready.' Then he said to a friend, 'Farewell; be diligent in duty, make 'your peace' with God through Christ. There is a great trial coming. As to the remnant I leave, I have committed them to God. Tell them from me not to weary nor be discouraged in maintaining the testimony, and the Lord will provide you teachers and ministers; and when He comes, He will make these despised truths glorious in the earth.'

For the Covenanters, Christ's Lordship was of supreme importance. Those who emerged from the crucible, when its heat was at its fiercest, displayed a faith of greater worth than gold. It has been proved genuine and will result in praise, glory and honour when Jesus Christ is revealed. That day will put all else into perspective.

Conclusion

What are we to conclude from this brief and selective study? Firstly, we should look beyond the heroism of our evangelical ancestors. Bravery has not been confined to them. Courage alone is no proof of truth. We should ask, 'What were the principles which governed their actions?' The Old Testament tells of a Reformation during the reign of Josiah, King of Judah. In the course of rebuilding the temple at Jerusalem, which had been destroyed by enemy action, a copy of the Scriptures was discovered. When the Jews examined it they realised that they had long ceased to act in accordance with God's law. This same process of re-evaluation was at the root of what happened during the sixteenth and seventeenth centuries. Men and women rediscovered that the Scriptures were the inspired word of God, and as such, had complete authority. They realised that scriptural teaching lay at the very heart of the Church and to the very nature of Christian worship. In the process, they also rediscovered the gospel itself. They came to realise that the established church was preaching a different gospel from that of the New Testament. Many suffered and died in order to reaffirm Biblical authority so that they – and we – might worship, not in a way which human tradition required, but the way in which God commanded.

This great tradition has been passed to us. We are heirs of a priceless heritage. We honour such men and women. We thank God for them, yet we are not to worship them. They made mistakes; they are not to be idolised or slavishly imitated. There is a danger in looking back to a Golden Age and wallowing in nostalgia. 'If only we could have been at Wittenburg or Geneva!' But we were not – we have to serve God in our day. We must aim to pass on the light of the Reformation candle to future generations. The God of Tyndale and Bunyan is our God! Christ continues to build His Church and will do so unto eternity!

In the letter to the Hebrews it is said that a great cloud of witnesses exists to encourage the people of God to run the race set before them. These brothers and sisters of ours may be physically dead but they are still speaking, and they tell us to keep running, to keep looking to Jesus and, like them, to endure as seeing Him who is invisible.

This was not easy for the biblical 'heroes' or those of Reformation days and will certainly not be easy for us either. Like the great reformers, we must stand by the complete authority of Scripture and reject any venture that involves joining with groups who have departed from God's word – no matter how well intentioned.

As evangelical men and women, the Word of God is our final authority, not dreams, visions, tongues, prophecies, feelings and providences. We have no mandate to experiment or innovate in worship; we must worship God in a way which is true to scripture and free from man made liturgy, as our biblically minded forefathers did. They looked into Scripture and saw hymns, spiritual songs, prayers and the reading and preaching of God's Word. That too, should be sufficient for us. Some people today deride and decry this 'tradional' worship. But it was – and is – a serious attempt to worship God in the way in which he decreed. If our worship is dead, it is not because of the structure or its origin!

Let us be proud of our heritage. We are part of a great multitude that no man can number. We are a people with roots – both in time and in eternity. One day the kingdoms of this world will become the kingdoms of our God and of his Christ. The earth will yet be filled with the glory of God as the waters cover the sea. In the meantime, there is a fight to be fought, a race to run, a crown to be won. The God of the Reformers and the Puritans is our refuge. This God is our God for ever!

Quotations and Bibliography

Quotations

1: Romans 15:4 (AV)
2: Knappen, 'Tudor Puritanism'
3: Ibid
4: Trevor Roper, 'Archbishop Laud'
5: Knappen, op. Cit.
6: Stephen Marshall (quoted by J.Lewis Wilson, Puritan Conference 1960)
7: Haller, 'The Rise of Puritanism'
8: Knappen, op. Cit.
9: C.V. Wedgwood, 'The King's Peace'
10: Ibid

Bibliography

Owen, 'The Reformation'
Rupp Drewery, 'Martin Luther'
R.H. Bainton, 'Here I Stand'
Francois Wendel, 'Calvin'
M.M. Knappen, 'Tudor Puritanism'
H.Trevor Roper 'Archbishop Laud'
C.V. Wedgwood 'The King's Peace'
A.S.P. Woodhouse 'Puritanism and Liberty'
William Haller 'The Rise of Puritanism'
Jock Purves 'Fair Sunshine'
Iain Murray 'The Banner of Truth Magazine'

Other Recommended Reading:
Brian Edwards, 'God's Outlaw'
J.H. Merle D'Aubigne, 'The Reformation in England'